MAR 1 5 2019   MAIN LIBRARY
ALBANY PUBLIC LIBRARY.

1·2·3
I Can Build!

Irene Luxbacher

KIDS CAN PRESS

ARCHITECTURE is the art of making the buildings we live, work and play in. Buildings come in all sorts of shapes and sizes and can be made from lots of different materials. Let's build houses and buildings …

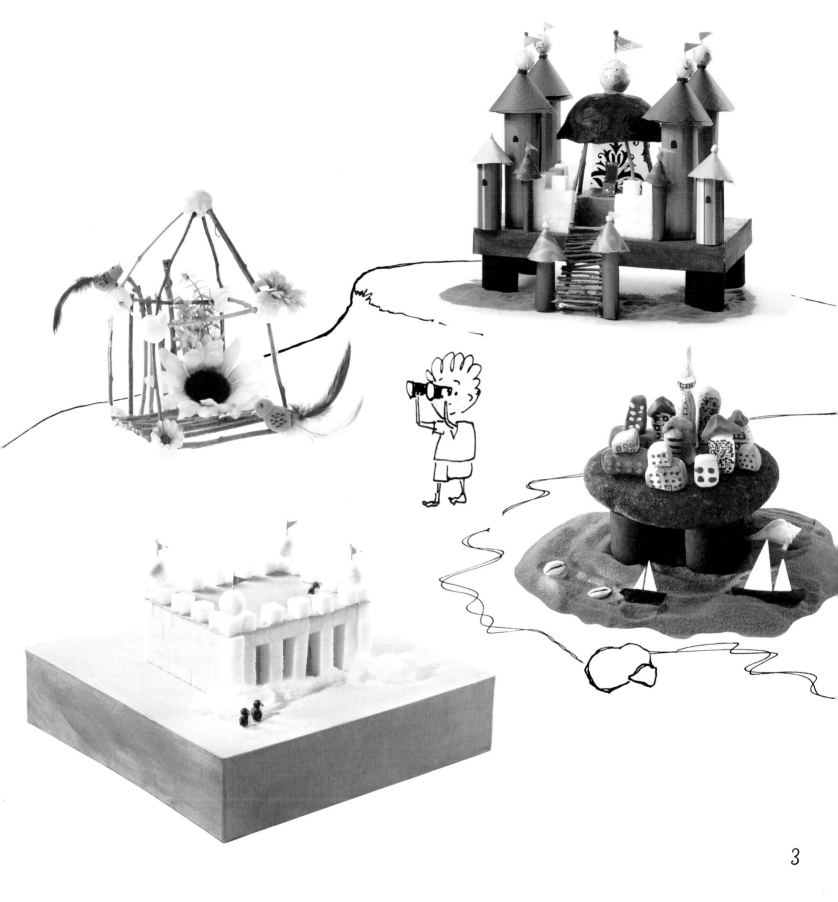

The things you use to build with are called

MATERIALS.

• CARDBOARD, SHOE BOXES,
JUICE CONTAINERS AND
CARDBOARD ROLLS

• FOUND OBJECTS,
SUCH AS BEADS,
BUTTONS, SHELLS,
TWIGS AND FLOWERS

• COLORED
PAPER

• WHITE GLUE AND
A SMALL PAINTBRUSH

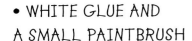

• SUGAR CUBES

• MODELING CLAY
(LIKE PLAY DOUGH
OR PLASTICINE)

• SCISSORS

• PAINT AND
PAINTBRUSHES

• WASHABLE
MARKERS

ARTIST'S SECRET:

Start a collection of all kinds of
boxes and other building materials.
Keep them all in one place so they're
always handy.

Standing STRONG

Just like you STAND STRONG on your two feet, a building needs a base to keep it steady. Make a strong base for your buildings to stand on and lay the groundwork for an amazing seaside city!

1. Cut two toilet paper rolls in half and paint them. Stand the four pieces up on end. Find something flat, such as the lid of a shoe box or a rock, to place on top of the rolls. This is your base. Carefully move the rolls around until the base doesn't wobble.

2. Roll, pinch or cut bits of modeling clay into lots of fun-looking little buildings. Use a marker or paint to add windows, bricks and doors on your buildings.

3. Put a drop of white glue on the bottom of each building to glue them to your city's base. Let them dry.

LAND HO!
A City by the Sea!

Place your mini city on some blue sand, cellophane or flattened modeling clay so it looks like it's surrounded by water. Sit ships made from paper cutouts on top of the water. Add a few seashells or fish molded from bits of modeling clay to finish off your city by the sea!

The base of a building is called the FOUNDATION. Often, the foundation is deep underground to help keep the building very steady.

Let's JOIN TOGETHER Now

Birds often build their homes using twigs they've found. Make like a bird, and join some twigs together to build a little house where a feathered friend might live.

1. Collect sixteen twigs that are about the size of a pencil. If some are too long, break or carefully cut them with a pair of scissors.

Roll eight small pieces of modeling clay into little balls about the size of your thumb.

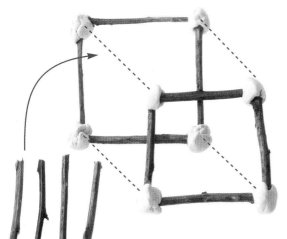

2. Join four twigs together using four of the balls of clay to make a square. Make another square with four more twigs and balls of clay. Connect the two squares by pressing another four twigs into the corners of each square to make a cube.

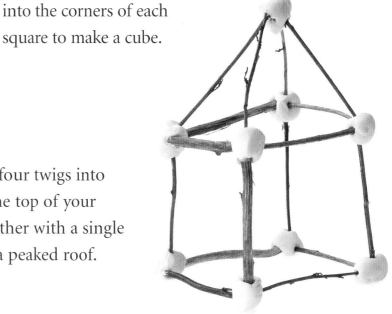

3. Press the last four twigs into the clay corners of the top of your cube. Join them together with a single ball of clay to make a peaked roof.

8

CHEEP, CHEEP!
A Breezy Birdhouse!

Glue more twigs onto your birdhouse to make
a floor and walls. Decorate your birdhouse
with leaves and flowers. Make a little bird
or two to live in your birdhouse using
colorful balls of modeling clay,
beads and feathers.
How tweet it is!

The skeleton of a building
(what a building looks like
before it has solid walls) is
called its STRUCTURE.

9

Put a LID on It!

Hey! It's a mini mansion that doubles as a terrific treasure box!
You never know what kind of treasures you'll find when you
LIFT THE LID on this gem of an idea.

1. Tear or cut some colorful tissue
paper into a pile of small strips or
squares. In a bowl, mix three big
spoonfuls of white glue with half
a cup of water.

2. Rub a small amount of petroleum jelly over
the outside of a small upside-down plastic bowl. Place
a strip of tissue paper on the bowl, and brush it with
some glue mixture. Repeat this step until the entire
bowl is covered in two or three layers of tissue paper.
Let it dry.

3. Paint a clean frozen juice container for
the bottom of your mushroom mansion. Let
it dry. (This is the part of your treasure box that
holds the treasure.) Carefully remove your dried
tissue paper lid from the plastic bowl and place
it on top of the painted juice container.

OH, MAN! A Mushroom Mansion!

Add a handle to your mushroom cap roof by gluing a large bead to the top. Glue on windows, a door and colorful paper polka dots. Use scraps of felt, pom-poms and modeling clay to make flowers and a friendly caterpillar that guards the treasures you keep in your mushroom mansion!

When a part of a building has a particular job to do, it has a FUNCTION. The function of your mushroom mansion's roof is to keep your treasures hidden and safe.

In the FOLD

Create this wild and wacky **HOUSE** one room at a time. This **PAPER PROJECT** has plenty of rooms with a view!

1. Fold a long strip of bristol board four times to make a rectangular or square room. Tape the ends. Fold another long strip of bristol board three times to make a triangular-shaped room. Tape the ends. Repeat until you have as many rooms as you like.

2. Place one folded room on a piece of colorful, patterned paper. Trace around the room with a pencil and cut the shape out. Tape the cut-out piece to the back of the room. Repeat for each room.

3. Stack and arrange your rooms one at a time using tape or glue to hold them in place. Make a few folds in a long strip of bristol board, and glue or tape it on top of your house for a zigzag roof.

TA-DA! A Delightful Dwelling!

Roll and pinch modeling clay to make furniture for your house, such as a couch or a table. Make more furniture for each of your rooms by folding small strips of construction paper or bristol board into a desk, chairs, a bed and whatever else your crazy, comfy house might need.

The inside of a building is called the INTERIOR. The outside of a building is called the EXTERIOR.

Stack 'EM Up

Sugar CUBES that have been glued together are the starting point of this cool-looking CASTLE. But remember, this home sweet home isn't for eating!

1. Glue together a row of nine sugar cubes. Next, glue together five stacks of three cubes. Let the glue dry. One at a time, glue each stack onto the row of cubes, spacing them one sugar-cube apart. Let the glue dry. Turn it upside down, and this is the first wall of your ice castle.

2. Glue together another row of nine sugar cubes. Glue three more rows of cubes on top of the first to make a solid wall. This is your second wall. Repeat this step two more times to make the last two walls. Let the glue dry.

3. Stand the walls up, and glue them together at the corners. Cut a piece of construction paper or bristol board for the roof of your ice castle and glue it in place. Let dry.

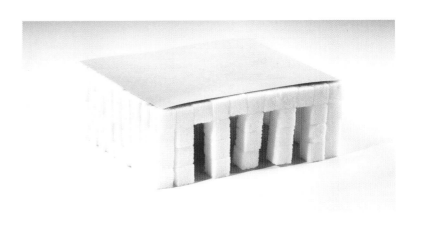

14

COOL! An Ice Castle!

Add more sugar cubes to the corners and along the top of your castle to give it a really royal-looking finish. Place it on top of a wintery blue-and-white background with cotton snowdrifts, plastic foam snowballs and a few friendly penguins made from modeling clay!

A standing post that helps hold up the walls or roof of a building, like the stacks of sugar cubes you made, is called a PILLAR.

HIGH in the SKY

Try turning some simple paper shapes into a **TALL TOWER** that's filled with fun!
It's a **BUILDING PROJECT** any high-flying acrobat would love to swing, slide and play in!

1. For the main part of your tower, cut a long rectangle out of construction paper or bristol board. Roll it up into a tube and tape the edges together.

2. Make a slide by drawing a spiral on a piece of construction paper, as shown. Cut along the spiral. Tape the center of the spiral to the top of the tube and let the rest wrap around to the bottom.

3. For the roof, trace around a large plate onto construction paper or bristol board, and cut it out. Draw and cut a straight line from the outside to the center of the circle. Slide one edge over the other to make a cone, and tape it in place. Set the cone on your tower.

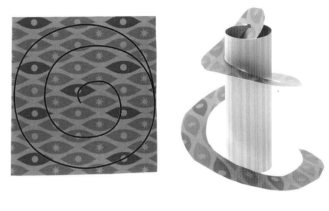

WHEE!
A Fabulous Fun House!

Make as many towers as you like and decorate them with foam balls, paper flags and acrobats that have been pinched out of bits of colorful modeling clay. What else would keep your acrobats happy while high in the sky in this fabulously fun house?

A building that stands taller than it is wide is called a TOWER.

A DREAM DESIGN

What would you make if you put all your **BUILDING TECHNIQUES** together into one **AMAZING IDEA**? What about a **PALACE** fit for a king or queen!

THE FOUNDATION

Paint four cardboard tubes and the lid of a shoe box. Place the lid on top of the four tubes, making sure your foundation doesn't wobble.

THE STRUCTURE

Roll eight small pieces of modeling clay into balls. Carefully cut or break twelve twigs so they're all about same size. Make a square by pressing the ends of four twigs into four balls of clay. Repeat. Use the last four twigs to join the two squares into a cube.

A THRONE ROOM

Cut a square piece of patterned paper or scrap of wallpaper and glue it onto the back wall of your twig structure. Place it on top of your foundation. Fold a small strip of construction paper into a chair. Decorate it with glitter or markers to make a throne. Set it on top of a small painted box inside the throne room.

WALLS

Glue a row of sugar cubes along the sides and back of the throne room. Glue another row of sugar cubes on top of the first. Repeat until your castle walls are as tall as you like.

THE ROOF

Find an old plastic bowl big enough to fit on top of your twig structure. Turn the bowl upside down and rub petroleum jelly on the outside. Place a piece of colorful tissue paper on the bowl and brush on some watered-down white glue. Repeat with more tissue. When it's dry, carefully remove the tissue roof from the bowl and place it on the throne room structure.

TALL TOWERS

Cut a long rectangle out of bristol board. Roll it into a tall tube and tape the edges. Trace around a can on another piece of bristol board. Cut the circle out and make another cut from the outside to the center of the circle. Slide one edge over the other to make a cone, and tape it in place. Place it on your tall tube. Make as many towers as you like.

A **PERFECT** Palace!

Decorate your palace with colorful paint, flags made out of toothpicks and scraps of paper, a bridge made out of leftover twigs and a watery-looking moat made from colored sand or paper scraps.

An **ARCHITECT** is someone who designs and helps construct buildings.

Note to PARENTS and TEACHERS

We chose a few simple structures as a way of exploring some basic building techniques, but there are lots of other types of building ideas you can use to inspire your young architect. Here are a few ideas to get you started.

• Build a tall skyscraper. Use a collection of boxes, such as large cardboard boxes, medium-sized boxes, shoe boxes and small jewelry boxes. Stack your boxes from largest to smallest, cutting out doors and painting on windows as you construct your building.

• Build an ancient pyramid. Start by making six stacks of six sugar cubes glued together. Once the glue has dried, glue the stacks together to make a six-by-six square. Let dry. Repeat this step, each time making a smaller square until the last square is two-by-two. Stack and glue the squares to make your pyramid. Finish it off with one single cube glued on top. Once all the glue is dry, paint your miniature pyramid a sandy brown color and place it on a base of sand.

Tips to ensure a GOOD BUILDING EXPERIENCE every time:

1. Use inexpensive materials and make sure your young architect's clothes and the work area are protected. This way it's all about the fun, not the waste and the mess.

2. Focus on the process rather than the end product. Make sure your young architect is relaxed and having fun with the information instead of expecting perfection every time.

3. Remind your young architect that mistakes are an artist's best friend. The most interesting building ideas and designs are often discovered by mistake.

BUILDING Words

ARCHITECT
page 20

FUNCTION
page 11

PILLAR
page 15

ARCHITECTURE
page 2

INTERIOR and EXTERIOR
page 13

STRUCTURE
page 9

FOUNDATION
page 7

MATERIALS
page 4

TOWER
page 17

FOR NOAH AND ELIJAH

Special thanks to Stacey Roderick and Karen Powers. This book would not have been possible without their amazing talents and insights.

Text and illustrations © 2009 Irene Luxbacher

All rights reserved. No part of this publication may be reproduced, stored in a retrieval system or transmitted, in any form or by any means, without the prior written permission of Kids Can Press Ltd. or, in case of photocopying or other reprographic copying, a license from The Canadian Copyright Licensing Agency (Access Copyright). For an Access Copyright license, visit www.accesscopyright.ca or call toll free to 1-800-893-5777.

Many of the designations used by manufacturers and sellers to distinguish their products are claimed as trademarks. Where those designations appear in this book and Kids Can Press Ltd. was aware of a trademark claim, the designations have been printed in initial capital letters. (e.g., Plasticine)

Neither the Publisher nor the Author shall be liable for any damage that may be caused or sustained as a result of conducting any of the activities in this book without specifically following instructions, conducting the activities without proper supervision or ignoring the cautions contained in the book.

Kids Can Press acknowledges the financial support of the Government of Ontario, through the Ontario Media Development Corporation's Ontario Book Initiative, and the Government of Canada, through the BPIDP, for our publishing activity.

Published in Canada by
Kids Can Press Ltd.
29 Birch Avenue
Toronto, ON M4V 1E2

Published in the U.S. by
Kids Can Press Ltd.
2250 Military Road
Tonawanda, NY 14150

www.kidscanpress.com

Kids Can Press is a Corus™ Entertainment company

Edited by Stacey Roderick
Designed by Karen Powers

All photos: Ray Boudreau
(except scissors: © iStockphoto.com/Mark Yuill)
Printed and bound in Singapore

The paper used to print this book was produced with elemental chlorine-free pulp, harvested from managed sustainable forests.

The hardcover edition of this book is smyth sewn casebound. The paperback edition of this book is limp sewn with a drawn-on cover.

CM 09 0 9 8 7 6 5 4 3 2 1
CM PA 09 0 9 8 7 6 5 4 3 2 1

Library and Archives Canada Cataloguing in Publication

Luxbacher, Irene, 1970–
    123 I can build! / written by Irene Luxbacher ; illustrated by Irene Luxbacher.

(Starting art)

ISBN 978-1-55453-316-9

1. Building—Technique—Juvenile literature. I. Title. II. Title: One, two, three I can build!. III. Series: Luxbacher, Irene, 1970– . Starting art.

TH149 L88 2009   j690   C2008-907054-2